TRUTHFORLIFE®
THE BIBLE-TEACHING MINISTRY OF **ALISTAIR BEGG**

The mission of Truth For Life is to teach the Bible with clarity and relevance so that unbelievers will be converted, believers will be established, and local churches will be strengthened.

Daily Program
Each day, Truth For Life distributes the Bible teaching of Alistair Begg across the U.S. and in several locations outside of the U.S. through 1,800 radio outlets. To find a radio station near you, visit **truthforlife.org/stationfinder**.

Free Teaching
The daily program, and Truth For Life's entire teaching archive of over 2,000 Bible-teaching messages, can be accessed for free online and through Truth For Life's full-feature mobile app. Download the free mobile app at **truthforlife.org/app** and listen free online at **truthforlife.org**.

At-Cost Resources
Books and full-length teaching from Alistair Begg on CD, DVD, and USB are available for purchase at cost, with no markup. Visit **truthforlife.org/store**.

Where to Begin?
If you're new to Truth For Life and would like to know where to begin listening and learning, find starting point suggestions at **truthforlife.org/firststep**. For a full list of ways to connect with Truth For Life, visit **truthforlife.org/subscribe**.

Contact Truth For Life
P.O. Box 398000 Cleveland, Ohio 44139
phone 1 (888) 588-7884   **email** letters@truthforlife.org
 /truthforlife   @truthforlife   truthforlife.org

P9-DUY-577

"Whether you find the cross of Christ a bit of puzzle or you want your heart to be filled with wonder all over again, *The Cross in Four Words* is a great book to go to. It's short and simple, but it takes us deep into the heart of the mystery of God's reconciling love."

Tim Chester, Pastor, Grace Church, Boroughbridge, UK; Faculty Member, Crosslands Training; Author, *Enjoying God*

"This is a really helpful book that I will be sharing widely. I read it in a single sitting and took a lot of notes."

Alistair Begg, Senior Pastor, Parkside Church, Cleveland, Ohio; Author, *Pray Big*

"We should never stop coming to the cross, marvelling at the wonder and kindness of God's plan of salvation. This important and accessible book helps us to do just that. It gives a spur to cross-shaped thinking and living that we are so in need of today and always."

Alex Weston, Senior Female Students Pastor, St Andrew the Great Church, Cambridge, UK

"The idea that God's wrath against our sin has to be poured out on his own Son is despised and ridiculed today. Yet it is the non-negotiable heart of the Christian gospel. In this book this great central truth is both defended and gloried in. It will sharpen your thinking and warm your heart. Highly recommended."

Paul Mallard, Pastor, Widcombe Baptist Church, Bath, UK

"A superb biblical theology in summary form of what God has done in and through Jesus Christ. It is refreshing to see complex theological categories such as redemption, justification and propitiation presented unapologetically and in such an accessible way. All three contributors bring a fresh and insightful approach. I recommend *The Cross in Four Words* to Christians and local churches both as a discipleship resource and as an excellent evangelistic tool."

Edwin Ewart, Principal, The Irish Baptist College

"This brilliant short book is at once deeply biblical and intensely practical, easily read, heart-warming and challenging: characteristic of each of the contributors' ministries. The cross is clearly explained and mission is faithfully defined and sharply applied—each peppered with great and fresh illustrations. This little book is excellent and worth bulk buying to give to new and older Christians alike. I love it and benefitted from it. It has caused me to praise God, again, for Christ's cross!"

Trevor Johnston, Rector, All Saints' Church, Belfast, UK; Chair, Irish Men's Convention

"If we forget the cross—or fail to understand our desperate need of its reconciling work—we will lose our joy. *The Cross in Four Words* redirects our gaze to "Christ crucified," reminding us of the love that bore our sin so that we might experience true freedom, forgiveness, justice, and purpose. This helpful book will refresh your heart and renew your mind in the wonder of such a great salvation."

Melissa Kruger, Director of Content, The Gospel Coalition; Author, *The Envy of Eve*

Freedom

Forgiveness

Justice

Purpose

THE CROSS
IN FOUR WORDS

thegoodbook.com | thegoodbook.co.uk
thegoodbook.com.au | thegoodbook.co.nz | thegoodbook.co.in

CONTENTS

INTRODUCTION
RICHARD COEKIN

T he preaching and ministry of the early Christians were dominated by one theme: "Christ crucified".

But proclaiming "Christ crucified" in the first century sounded absurd. "Christ" means "anointed one" and refers to God's chosen Saviour King, promised long ago by his Old Testament prophets, and expected to arrive with irresistible power and glory. But "crucified" refers to the Roman punishment of criminals by crucifixion—designed to be the most hideously cruel and obscenely humiliating death imaginable. To proclaim "Christ crucified" sounded ridiculous—like advertising "dry water".

In fact, the apostle Paul himself describes this message as a "stumbling-block" (something disgusting) to those from his own Jewish background and "foolishness" (something insane) to those from other nations:

Jews demand signs and Greeks look for wisdom, but we preach Christ crucified: a stumbling-block to Jews and

foolishness to Gentiles, but to those whom God has called,
both Jews and Greeks, Christ the power of God and the
wisdom of God.   *(1 Corinthians 1 v 22-24)*[1]

Indeed, the message of Christ crucified remains a stumbling-block and foolishness in the world around us today.

Back then, Paul says, "Jews demand[ed] signs" because they respected impressive power and influence. They longed for a mighty warrior to liberate them from Roman occupation and they loved their spectacular temple religion. It's similar today. Our world ranks people by their social power and influence and by what they earn or own. Our culture is fascinated by celebrities and royalty. Our chat shows feature people because they're famous, not because they're good. And those from religious backgrounds tend to admire leaders who are powerful and popular, like the Pope. It's as difficult now as it was in Paul's day to admire a man who thought he had to die in agony and degradation on a cross for our sins. And it's hard to respect the churches who proclaim him. Then and now, the message of Christ crucified seems an offensive stumbling-block to many.

And back then, Paul says, "Greeks look[ed] for wisdom" because the Greco-Roman world respected impressive learning that brings successful living. The culture of the day fostered admiration for religious philosophers who were brilliant scholars and entertaining orators. Again, things are not so different today. Our world admires distinguished education and eminent qualifications. We prefer spiritual

[1] In this chapter, Bible quotations are taken from the NIV.

gurus who write bestselling books promising wellbeing without challenging our morality, like the Dalai Lama. It's as counter-cultural now as it was then to admire a tradesman from Galilee who warns of hell and divides public opinion. And many find it hard to respect Christians who follow him. Then and now, the message of Christ crucified seems like insane foolishness to many.

For example, the brilliant but atheistic Oxford biologist, Richard Dawkins, writes about Jesus' death in his bestselling book, *The God Delusion*, in these scornful terms:

> "*I have described atonement, the central doctrine of Christianity, as vicious, sadomasochistic and repellent. We should also dismiss it as barking mad.*" *(page 253)*

God's "atonement", his reconciliation of sinners to himself on the cross, is clearly a stumbling-block and foolishness to Dawkins. He hasn't realised that the cross isn't about God being horribly "sadomasochistic"—inviting pain because he likes it—but wonderfully self-sacrificial for others. He hasn't realised that the cross is not revealing God as "barking mad" but as passionately loving.

Christ crucified will always be a stumbling-block and foolishness to many—perhaps offensive and ridiculous to some of our family, or pathetic and stupid to some of our friends. And yet Christ crucified is what they need to hear about more than anything else. Because Paul goes on to explain that God has deliberately chosen the crucifixion of Christ as the means of our salvation in order to contradict and shame our proud assumptions about ourselves. He always planned to reveal his divine power and wisdom in a salvation that seems strange and confusing to us, so that we have to abandon our self-confidence and trust him instead. Paul says the message of "Christ crucified" is actually "the power of God and wisdom of God"—his effective and coherent way to save people from all nations who turn from sin to trust in Jesus.

THE CROSS THROUGHOUT THE SCRIPTURES

Many Christians may feel familiar with the basics of Christ crucified. But the more we can understand about the cross, the more we'll delight in God's amazing grace, and the better we'll be able to explain it to unbelieving family, friends and colleagues.

Christ crucified is central to Christianity. The cross is the purpose of creation and the turning point of history, the climax of Scripture and the heart of our faith. It is the highest revelation of God's glory and the deepest joy of our eternity—for ever stirring the vast crowds of heaven to worship the Lamb of God who was slain (Revelation 5 v 6-10)!

And the cross saturates the pages of Scripture from start to finish. For example, one word used for the cross (translated "cross" in Acts 10 v 39 and "pole" in Galatians 3 v 13) is also used at the beginning of Scripture, in the Garden of Eden, for the "tree of life" keeping God's people alive (Genesis 2 v 9). At the end, in Revelation 22 v 2, in a beautiful vision of God's new creation, the same "tree of life" is there to heal and sustain God's people for ever. This language points to the fact that Christ crucified is the centre of everything.

Surveying the whole of Scripture, we find that by his death, Christ has glorified his Father in many marvellous ways—too many to describe in detail here. For example, his death completed an exemplary Christian life that shows us how to live. His death disarmed Satan's claims upon us by suffering the penalty we deserve under God's law. And his death has saved us into a new humanity.

But the supreme accomplishment of Jesus' death was in satisfying God's holy justice. He accepted onto himself, like a lightning conductor, all God's anger against our sin. By faith in him, our sin is no longer counted against us.

The background which explains this wondrous accomplishment is found in three unfolding themes, beautiful crimson threads, flowing throughout the Old Testament. This is why the risen Jesus himself turned to the Old Testament to explain his death to his bewildered disciples on the road to the village of Emmaus:

"How foolish you are, and how slow to believe all that the prophets have spoken! Did not the Messiah have to suffer these things and then enter his glory?" And beginning with Moses and all the Prophets, he explained what was said in all the Scriptures concerning himself.
(Luke 24 v 25-27)

Paul, too, emphasised the importance of the cross in the Scriptures when he wrote:

> *For what I received I passed on to you as of first importance: that Christ died for our sins according to the Scriptures.*
> *(1 Corinthians 15 v 3)*

We will marvel more at the beauty of the cross, and be able to explain "Christ crucified" more clearly to others, when we follow these three crimson threads through the Old Testament to discover how the death of Christ brings us *freedom*, *forgiveness* and *justice*.

FREEDOM

Most people long for freedom of some kind—perhaps freedom from social constraints, political oppression or personal addictions. But the Scriptures reveal that true freedom begins with liberation from sin in order to serve God—through the sacrificial death of Jesus. This is called "redemption".

The background to our redemption for freedom is found in the account of the Passover in Exodus 12. Here we learn how God redeemed his people from slavery to Pharaoh and from the danger of death through the blood of a lamb, giving them the joyful freedom of worshipping him.

This points forward to the cross, where God redeemed us from slavery to sin through the blood of Jesus. The cross gains for us the joyful freedom of worshipping him with our whole lives.

FORGIVENESS

Many of us are familiar with the crushing feelings of guilt and fear that something we've done, or repeatedly done, has permanently ruined a relationship. But the Scriptures reveal that if we are willing to turn from our sin, God has made it possible to forgive all our sins—however dreadful they are—and restore our relationship with him.

The background to this forgiveness of sins is found in the account of the Day of Atonement celebrations in Leviticus 16. Here we learn how God cleansed his people from their guilt through rituals involving the blood of one goat and the banishment of another (a "scapegoat"). This averted his anger (this is technically called "propitiation") and gave them the privilege of access to the Lord's presence.

Again, this points forward to the cross, where God cleansed us from our sin through Jesus' bloodshed and banishment to hell as our scapegoat, giving us the huge relief of total forgiveness and the privilege of constant access to God in heaven as forgiven people.

JUSTICE

We all have a strong impulse to try to justify ourselves when we face accusation for getting things wrong. The Scriptures show us firstly that we are guilty of many sins, and on our own we could not expect to be declared righteous by God on his day of judgment. But secondly, they also reveal that God has provided a way for us to be justly declared righteous in his sight. This is called being "justified" by God's grace through faith in Jesus.

The background to this justification is found in many places, perhaps most wonderfully in the account of God's Suffering Servant in Isaiah 53. Here we learn how God planned to justly qualify his people for heaven despite our guilt under God's law. This would be done through an innocent servant who would be punished for our sins and raised to life to qualify his people for heaven with his righteous Christian life, lived for them.

Again, this points forward to the cross, where God completed in Jesus the perfect life of righteousness we all need. This righteousness is "imputed" to us—counted as our own—to qualify us for heaven without compromising God's perfect justice.

The following chapters will explore these wonderful aspects of the cross of Christ more fully. But there is one simple truth in all of these great passages which makes them easier to understand.

SWAPPING PLACES

Each of these passages involves a simple sacrificial exchange: a swap. The Passover lamb, the Day of Atonement goats and the Suffering Servant all point forward to Christ sacrificially swapping places with his people on the cross. God the Son became one of us, an ordinary man, so he could swap places with us on the cross. There he was treated as if he were us, suffering all the punishment of torment, shame and hell that we deserve—so we can be treated as if we were him, qualified to inherit in heaven as holy children of God. All these passages involve a simple, beautiful exchange. Jesus came to swap places with us.

Let me illustrate this by telling you about the extraordinary heroism of Bill Deacon. He was the winchman of an Air-Sea Rescue helicopter operating out of Bristow in the Shetland Islands, northeast of the Scottish mainland. In November 1997, the Green Lily cargo vessel was grounded on rocks and breaking up amidst mountainous waves. Lifeboats had been sent, but they could no longer get to the stricken vessel to save the crew trapped on board. Bill Deacon realised the only hope of saving the men was to descend from the helicopter himself onto the ship. Once on the deck, in terrible conditions, he attached each of the ten crew to his winch and they were raised up to safety in the helicopter in his place.

But as the last two men were lifted to safety, Bill Deacon himself was swept off the ship by a huge wave. His body was recovered the following day. He was posthumously awarded the George Medal for his courage.

In the same way, Christ came down from heaven to rescue his people in peril. Unlike Bill Deacon, Jesus was not merely *risking* his life for the sake of others. He came knowing for certain that he would have to die after suffering not only physically, but spiritually—draining the cup of his Father's wrath like a goblet of acid into his soul—to bring us the freedom, forgiveness and justice we need.

Why would Jesus do such a crazy thing? Because despite everything, Jesus loves us... passionately! For God to *allow* such a sacrifice is grace; for God to *provide* such a sacrifice is amazing grace; for God to *become* such a sacrifice is grace beyond our wildest dreams.

Freedom, forgiveness and justice. Three words that hint at how God has addressed the deepest hurts in our hearts and the greatest problems of our world. Three beautiful words that begin to flood our hearts with joy about "Christ crucified". Three exciting words that the chapters of this book will explore, explain and apply to our lives today.

And there is a fourth word.

PURPOSE

In the final chapter, we will hear Jesus' call in Mark 8 to follow him in a selfless life like his. To deny ourselves, take up our cross and follow him—not in pointless self-denial but for the salvation of the lost. This is why our fourth word is *purpose*. In a world full of people crying out to know who they are and why they exist, the cross of Christ fills our lives and our churches with the all-consuming mission and deeply satisfying purpose for which we have been created and re-created: to pick up our own cross and follow Jesus in a life of sacrificial service for the salvation of others.

As Christians we seek to love the people around us in every way that the Bible commands. We resist injustice, prejudice and ecological irresponsibility; we seek relief for victims of crime, poverty and trafficking; we contend for freedom of speech, protection of the unborn and the reformation of church denominations. But the most precious gift we have to offer the people of this world and the communities where we live is the life-saving message of "Christ crucified". It is the power of God to save sinners from the horrors of hell, for the holiness of heaven, in happiness for ever.

So read on and gaze with us in wonder at "Christ crucified ... the power of God and the wisdom of God"... in four words.

NOTE: This book began as a series of talks at REVIVE, the annual festival of Co-Mission, a church-planting and strengthening network in London. These churches are united in their determination to help bring the glorious message of "Christ crucified" to all the communities of their city.

THE STORY BEGINS

The Old Testament story that defined God's relationship with his people more than any other was the exodus. Long before, God had promised many, many descendants to Abraham. Now this promise was being fulfilled and there were enough to make a nation. But at the opening of the book of Exodus, this huge family was enslaved to the Egyptians. In Exodus 6 v 6-7, God promised to free them and to make them his own people. He would redeem them for himself.

The Passover was the fulfillment of that promise. God sent a series of plagues against the Egyptians to persuade them to release the Israelites, but they refused. The last plague was the death of the firstborn of every household. This would finally force the Egyptians to free the slaves.

In order to escape falling under the same curse, God told the Israelites to sacrifice lambs and smear the blood on their doorposts. The angel of death would then "pass over" and no one in those houses would die. Meanwhile, they were to get ready to leave the land of Egypt. We read of God's instructions for the Passover in Exodus 12.

1. FREEDOM

HOW GOD REDEEMS HIS PEOPLE
KEVIN DEYOUNG

Your mistakes will always be with you. That's what our world says.

Supposedly, we live in a time of moral relativism; but if you spend any time on the internet, you'll know we don't really have very many moral relativists. It is merciless: a place of guilt, shame, and Twitter mobs. If you have said the wrong thing on social media—if you posted the wrong thing when you were 16 years old—it will be forever recorded in digital history. Some employer sometime is going to find it, or new acquaintances are going to look back through your profile and see it, and so you can never escape your past. Your mistakes will always be with you. There are no do-overs.

And we all have a past, don't we? Social media just exaggerates the problem that has always been there. We've all made mistakes. We've all said or done the wrong thing at some point. We're all sinners.

Imagine someone set up a big screen for all your friends and neighbors, and invited them to watch your whole life—all you've looked at, all you've done, all you've said, all you've thought. If you're anything like me, you'd be tearing it down. You'd do all you could to stop them watching. It doesn't matter how many things we've done that may seem impressive; none of us would want everything in our past displayed on a screen for all to see.

But in 1 Corinthians 5 v 7-8, Paul tells his readers that they have had a new beginning. They are no longer like old bread, made with "the leaven of malice and evil."[2] Instead they can be "new" and "unleavened." They can put aside their past mistakes and look to an entirely new future.

I have a New future in Christ.

Why? Paul says that this new beginning takes place because "Christ, our Passover lamb, has been sacrificed." Jesus has died on the cross to save us from our sins. And so, as Christians, we understand what the world does not: that you can start over. We are the people of God set free from sin, and our past does not define us.

To see the nature of this freedom—what we are set free from, what we are set free for, and how we are set free—we need to look more closely at Exodus 12, where God gives instructions for the Passover sacrifice, that forerunner of the greater sacrifice thousands of years later.

[2] In this chapter, Bible quotations are taken from the ESV.

A NEW BEGINNING

The exodus was the supreme event in the history of the nation of Israel. It was the turning point. It was a new beginning.

Here are God's first instructions:

> *This month shall be for you the beginning of months. It shall be the first month of the year for you. Tell all the congregation of Israel that on the tenth day of this month every man shall take a lamb according to their fathers' houses, a lamb for a household. And if the household is too small for a lamb, then he and his nearest neighbor shall take according to the number of persons; according to what each can eat you shall make your count for the lamb.*
> *(Exodus 12 v 2-4)*

The Israelites were a slave people and so their time was not their own. But now God was marking out a new time. That is why he says, "This month shall be the beginning of months for you." They are starting a new calendar. The Passover would mark the end of life as they knew it in Egypt and a new beginning as the nation of Israel.

This is the first time in Exodus that the word translated "congregation" is used. They have been called "Hebrews," and they have been called "sons of Israel," but now, uniquely, they are called a community, a congregation—no longer slaves but a people, a nation. They can share lambs between households because there is a fundamental unity in this one body.

They are starting out as a new nation, with a new identity, a new name, and a new beginning. They get to start over. They are free.

FREED BY FAITH

The instructions God gives to his people on the night of the Passover reveal that one key to their freedom is an attitude of faith.

> *The whole assembly of the congregation of Israel shall kill their lambs at twilight. Then they shall take some of the blood and put it on the two doorposts and the lintel of the houses in which they eat it. They shall eat the flesh that night, roasted on the fire; with unleavened bread and bitter herbs they shall eat it ... In this manner you shall eat it: with your belt fastened, your sandals on your feet, and your staff in your hand. And you shall eat it in haste. It is the LORD's Passover.*   (Exodus 12 v 6-8, 11)

Think about the faith that it took not only to move out from Egypt but to move out in haste. They had been slaves for 430 years (v 40) but now, suddenly, they had to be quick. No hesitation. By faith they understood: *Now is the time.*

Looking at what happened later in the story reveals what a big deal this step of faith was for the Israelites. In the rest of the book of Exodus, they are often grumbling. In just a matter of weeks after the Passover, they're pining for all they had left behind. "We sat by the meat pots and ate bread to the full," they complain (16 v 3). And again in

Numbers 11 v 5: "We remember the fish we ate in Egypt ... the cucumbers, the melons, the leeks, the onions, and the garlic."

The cucumbers? That seems like a serious lack of perspective. But you can understand it, because slavery was all these people had ever known. It was not a good life, but it was their life. They had a rhythm and a routine. They knew what to expect. They knew what today, tomorrow, and even next year would hold for them. Someone gave them food, gave them purpose, and told them what to do. At least it was understandable.

That was why, in the wilderness, they longed to go back. They would rather have the bondage they knew than trust the God they could not see. They wished they had not accepted God's redemption.

But at the start of their journey, in Exodus 12, they did have the faith to recognize that they needed freedom and that now they had the chance to gain it. In verse 28, we read, "As the LORD had commanded Moses and Aaron, so they did." They obeyed all that they had been told. They stepped out in faith. And they found freedom.

FREE TO WORSHIP

Imagine that first day, waking up and being able to say, *I can do what I want to do. I can decide for myself. I don't have to make bricks!* The Israelites would have their own land and be their own nation. They were free.

But this was not freedom as our world would understand freedom.

Being whoever you want to be is a very Western ideal. People talk at length about sexual freedom or lifestyle freedom. "You can choose. You decide. Don't let anyone else tell you what to do or think or be." That is what we are told.

The Bible gives us a different way of talking about freedom. Real freedom is not the ability to be whoever you *want* to be. Real freedom is the ability to be who you *ought* to be. There is a right way to live. This means that there is a purpose to our freedom.

A key point in the story of Exodus is the moment when Moses comes into Pharaoh's court to give him God's message. We generally think of it as very dramatic. He marches in, voice booming: *Let. My. People. Go.* Over and over, the same bald assertion: *Let us go.* But we often forget the rest of what Moses said. He said, "Thus says the LORD, the God of Israel: 'Let my people go, that they may hold a feast to me in the wilderness'" (Exodus 5 v 1).

The goal of freedom, in other words, was worship. Being free from slavery under the Egyptians meant being in servitude to God. When the Israelites got into the wilderness, they would receive the law that would tell them how to live: how to serve and worship God.

But notice that serving God is not like serving the Egyptians. God doesn't force people to serve him in order to gain his protection or help. Receiving the law comes *after* the salvation that is freely given by God.

When the people cried out for help, God didn't come and say, *Okay, you're slaves. I might be able to help. But what I'll do is give you ten commandments. I'm going to check back in a year to see how you're doing with the commandments. If you're hitting about 80% of them, then I've got some plagues up my sleeve to help you; but let me just see how you're doing first.*

No, that's not how salvation works. That's not how redemption works. What God said was "I am the LORD your God" (Exodus 6 v 7). He accepted them as his people before they had done anything to deserve it. He saved them by his own gracious mercy, and then he gave them the law. And the law was not somehow to imprison them but to keep them free.

Imagine you're driving on some hairpin turn at the edge of a mountain, and there's a great precipice beside you. If you see a guardrail between your car and that precipice, what do you say to yourself? You don't say, "I hate these guardrails. I hate being told what to do." No, you say, "That's a good idea. I could get hurt here. I'm grateful that somebody thought of this." Those guardrails keep you safe by showing you where to go. They keep you free.

It is the same with God's law: it is given to God's people not to enslave them again but to keep them free. To do whatever we want to do is not real freedom because we will choose slavery, just as the Israelites wanted to do in the desert. We will end up enslaved to the way others think of us. We will choose to be slaves to our own aspirations. Or we will allow our past mistakes to master us and determine our future. But to do as God would have us do is real freedom because he knows what is right.

Being free to worship God is good because of who God is. In Exodus 12 v 12 God says:

> On all the gods of Egypt I will execute judgments: I am the LORD.

Whenever you see "LORD" in those small capital letters, it is indicating that in the original Hebrew this is the divine name, the name God gave himself when he spoke to Moses in Exodus 3 v 1: Yahweh (or, in older translations, Jehovah). It means "I am that I am." Not just any god, but God himself. The purpose of the ten plagues was to defeat Egypt's gods and show to Israel and the whole world that the LORD was God, and the LORD alone.

Each of those plagues struck at something that represented one of the Egyptian gods or goddesses. They had a goddess of the Nile, another of frogs, another of livestock. Over and over again, the plagues were God's way of saying that those so-called gods and goddesses were not God. *They're not God. They're not God. They're not God.* Only the LORD is worthy of worship. And following him is the way to be truly free. That is the redemption that Jesus Christ later died to give.

FREE FROM DEATH

The Passover sacrifice did what God promised it would: it caused the Egyptian Pharaoh to free his slaves. Out came the Israelites into the wilderness, ready to worship the God who had saved them.

But deliverance from physical bondage was not the only freedom the Israelites needed. Nor is it the most important freedom that we need.

In Hebrews 2 v 15 another type of slavery is brought to our attention. Jesus went to the cross to "deliver all those who through fear of death were subject to lifelong slavery."

People have always been in bondage to the fear of death. We exercise and we eat healthily and we take pills and we do whatever we can because we are desperate to keep living. Yet when you step back from this, you realize the truth. One out of one persons will die. Every one of us.

If you want real freedom, lasting freedom, lifelong freedom, you need a way to solve the problem of death.

The Egyptians were slaves to this fear too. So many of their gods were about crops and fertility and health and safe passage in death. They had a whole pantheon of deities to help them manage death and feel protected from it. But God, the LORD God, conquered all these deities. The last of the plagues, the killing of the firstborn, showed the Egyptians that their gods could not set them free from death. They eventually set the Israelites free because they were so afraid:

For they said, "We shall all be dead."   *(Exodus 12 v 33)*

But the Passover also showed that there is one God who *can* set you free from the fear of death.

> *For the LORD will pass through to strike the Egyptians, and when he sees the blood on the lintel and on the two doorposts, the LORD will pass over the door and will not allow the destroyer to enter your houses to strike you.*
> *(Exodus 12 v 23)*

The Israelites are to select a lamb on the tenth day of the first month (v 3); they are to kill those lambs at twilight on the fourteenth day (v 6); and they are to put the blood on the doorpost and on the lintel of their houses so that the angel of death will pass over (v 7, 13). The sacrifice of the lamb takes the place of the firstborn in their households. By making this sacrifice, they can be freed from death.

This might seem unfair to the Israelites. After all, they've been the oppressed: it's the Egyptians who have been the oppressors. They might have been excused for thinking that the Egyptians were the bad guys and they were the good guys. But now they too are threatened with death. They too are subject to God's judgment unless they make this sacrifice. They need to be saved. Why? The truth is that the Israelites are sinners too.

Sin means turning away from God. It means refusing to worship him and live according to his law. It means choosing slavery to other things. It means dismantling those guardrails on the edge of the precipice. It leads to death.

It is not that the world has bad guys and good guys, the oppressors and the oppressed, and only the bad oppressors deserve judgment. No: everyone, every single person, is guilty of sin and enslaved to death. This is why the Israelites had to make the Passover sacrifice. Already, at the very beginning of their history as a nation, God was impressing upon his people this singular truth: a lamb must die if you will live.

OUR PASSOVER LAMB

Hopefully it's not hard to connect the dots from that first Passover lamb to the cross, which is what Paul does in 1 Corinthians 5. "Christ [is] our Passover lamb" (v 7) because we find in the cross and in the empty tomb all of these same realities.

For the Israelites, trusting in the blood of the lamb, smeared on the doorposts, meant that death would pass over them. For us, trusting in the blood of the Lamb, shed on the cross, means that death will also pass over us.

The Israelites put their faith in the lamb and confidently got ready for a new life. As followers of Jesus, we put our faith in the Lamb and confidently get ready for eternal life.

We have, at the cross, a new beginning. A new beginning for Jesus, who would rise from the dead. A new beginning for the disciples, who were sent into the world. A new beginning for the world as it started to hear that message. And a new beginning for you.

That is why Paul tells us to be like a "new" batch of bread—"as you really are" (1 Corinthians 5 v 7). We are not striving to become new; we *are* new. Elsewhere Paul repeats the same idea: "If anyone is in Christ, he is a new creation" (2 Corinthians 5 v 17). You have a new beginning. You have a new freedom. Romans 6 tells us that we are no longer slaves to wickedness and sin but that we are now slaves to ever-increasing righteousness.

Our world says that you can't help being who you are. Identity is vitally important because that is what you operate out of. Are you male or female? Are you black or white? What are you? That's your identity. In the words of Lady Gaga, we are "born this way." You can only be what you were born as, and that's something you can't help. Your own sense of identity is what you should celebrate.

But this is only half right.

Paul says over and over again in different ways, *Be who you are.* So, who are we? What we understand as Christians is that while we may have all sorts of identities, the one that matters most and that is most fundamental is whether or not we are *in Christ*—whether or not we have put our faith in his sacrifice and have been freed by him.

We are born this way: born sinners, born into slavery. But the good news of the gospel is that you can be born *again*, born a different way. You have a new beginning, a new freedom, and a new forgiveness.

BETWEEN THE PASSOVER AND THE CROSS

There is one more thing to note here about the sacrifice of Jesus, and that is the *difference* between the cross and the Passover sacrifice. The cross fulfills what the Passover lamb prefigured. Jesus' sacrifice frees us forever.

God had purchased the Israelites for himself. They belonged to him. But, as we have seen, the Israelites had not only been in slavery to the Egyptians. They were also enslaved by sin. And so they had to keep on making sacrifices. The law described how sacrificing animals would atone for the people's sins. The priest would lay a hand upon the animal so as to say, *The guilt is upon the head of the substitute* (Leviticus 1 v 4). The animal would take the place of the guilty person so that the guilty person could become free—free to worship God again.

But these sacrifices had to be made again and again, because again and again the people failed to serve God and live as they ought. And even if there was a moment when the altar was empty, the priests were to keep the coals burning constantly and never let the flame go out (Leviticus 6 v 12-13). Century after century, God's people would have seen the fire coming up from the altar; year after year, gathered in the tabernacle, they would have seen another one of their sheep be brought to the slaughter and smelled in the air that sharp aroma of blood. Over and over throughout Israel's history, day after day, they were meant to be reminded that they were sinners in need of a Savior.

✄ FREED FOREVER

But finally there came a wild-eyed prophet eating bugs in the wilderness. His name was John the Baptist, and when he saw Jesus, he pointed to him and said, "Behold, the Lamb of God, who takes away the sin of the world!" (John 1 v 29).

What he meant was: *That man will put an end to all of this.* The cross of Christ did not just pay for one debt. It paid for all our debts and so redeemed us from sin permanently. Jesus is the fulfillment of all that was prefigured in the story of the exodus. In him we have a new beginning and a new freedom—and, crucially, we have them forever.

God doesn't look at the way we behave and say, *There you go again. You're going to need a really good week of obedience now if you want to retain your status as my son or daughter.* No, we are free from bondage to sin in the same way that the Israelites were free from physical bondage. We have been redeemed. We have been purchased by the blood of Christ, and now we belong to him.

This is the great paradox of Christianity. You no longer have a debt to be paid, but you belong to another. You've been purchased, which means you must say of yourself, *I don't owe, but I am not my own.* You are free, and yet at the same time you are God's servant. Can you hold both of those things? Our world can't. Our world either says you have to earn redemption, work for it, pull yourself up by your bootstraps and prove to God that you're worthy of being purchased by him; or it says that you are free and now you can do whatever you want, because God doesn't care—

he's just like a benevolent Santa Claus looking down and giving out gifts.

But both these views are wrong. One of the most countercultural passages in all the Bible is this:

You are not your own, for you were bought with a price. So glorify God in your body. (1 Corinthians 6 v 19-20)

It's not your body. It's not your life. It's his. At the cross, you have been redeemed. You have been purchased from slavery. You have been set free: set free to serve God, which is the only kind of freedom worth living for.

QUESTIONS FOR DISCUSSION

1. When have you wished for a new beginning?

2. What freedoms do people you know long for?

3. How is biblical freedom different from the way the world normally talks about freedom?

4. Why did the Israelites need to sacrifice a lamb?

5. What does the story of the Passover teach us about what it means to be redeemed by Christ?

6. What are the key differences between the Passover and the cross?

7. If you belong to God, how should you act?

THE STORY CONTINUES

After the Israelites got out of Egypt, Moses led them to Mount Sinai, where the presence of the Lord descended. The Israelites knew that this God was the one who had rescued them from slavery, who loved them and thought of them as his treasured child. But the effect of his presence was terrifying.

> *Mount Sinai was wrapped in smoke because the LORD had descended on it in fire. The smoke of it went up like the smoke of a kiln, and the whole mountain trembled greatly.*
> *(Exodus 19 v 18)*

It is here that God gives Moses instructions about how the Israelites are going to operate as a nation. This includes the fact that God is going to dwell among his people, within their camp.

God gives instructions to build an ark, a box of wood overlaid in gold and covered with a "mercy seat", which will be the place where, from then on, God will meet and speak with Moses (Exodus 25 v 10-22). This ark is to be kept in the Holy Place, a special section of the tented temple which the people are to build. The presence of God, which on Mount Sinai had been a huge fire combined with an earthquake and a storm, would be there, in the midst of Israel.

2. FORGIVENESS

HOW GOD PROVIDES PROPITIATION FOR SIN

YANNICK CHRISTOS-WAHAB

Nobody's perfect. As people, we all mess up. We know what it is to sin against other people and what it's like to be sinned against. Dealing with offence is an everyday issue because when we sin, it affects our relationships with one another. Sometimes these are things we can simply overlook, like when someone accidentally nudges you on the street or cuts you off in traffic. But even minor things can really affect our relationships. If you irritate someone, they will be less likely to want to spend time with you. And what do you do when someone has really hurt you—or when you have really hurt someone else?

We can try to resolve it by taking out our anger on them, but this often only leads to an endless cycle of vengeance. We can try to ignore it, but this becomes harder the more serious the offence is. Plus, it seems unjust to simply forget it. How do we deal with anger, justified anger, when people offend us or when we offend people? How can we both acknowledge the seriousness of the offence and restore the relationship so that the damage is healed?

We all know what an important problem this is when it comes to human relationships. But it is a far more important problem when it comes to our relationship with God. God is our Creator and the source of all of life, but we have offended him by turning away from him in endless different ways. This means that he is angry with us, and our relationship with him is damaged. If we are to be restored to a proper relationship with God, something must be done about his anger towards us. We need him to forgive us.

Unsurprisingly, as the Israelites travelled through the desert and as they established themselves in the promised land, God's presence continued to be terrifying and dangerous. This was the God who had rescued the Israelites, who loved them, and whom they wanted to worship. But this was also the God who was angry with their sin and whose holy nature was like a consuming fire. Whenever anyone approached him, they would die, he warned (Exodus 19 v 10-12, 21-22). So how could the people cope with God's presence in their midst? How could they find acceptance from the God they could not approach?

Leviticus 16 supplies the answer to this question. It describes God's instructions for the Day of Atonement, when the high priest was to atone for all of the people's sin: literally to make them "at one" with God, forgiven by him for their sin, and able to dwell with him without fear.

This was a major festival for the Israelite people, a series of rituals that they were to perform every single year. It was as big a part of their calendar as Christmas is for us.

And it is just as relevant to us as it was to them, however strange its details may seem (and they are quite strange). By looking at the Day of Atonement, we can see why sin is such a big deal and what consequences it has for our relationship with God. We can see God's amazing mercy in providing a way for people to gain forgiveness. And we can see what kind of sacrifice had to be made in order to find the solution for sin.

The Day of Atonement was always intended to point forward to the death of Jesus on the cross. It was meant to prepare God's people for someone who would finally take away sin, grant forgiveness and generously welcome them—and us—into God's presence.

FIRST, A WARNING

Leviticus 16 starts by reminding us of the seriousness of God's anger against sin:

> The LORD spoke to Moses after the death of the two sons of Aaron, when they drew near before the LORD and died, and the LORD said to Moses, "Tell Aaron your brother not to come at any time into the Holy Place inside the veil, before the mercy seat that is on the ark, so that he may not die. For I will appear in the cloud over the mercy seat."
> (Leviticus 16 v 1-2)[3]

[3] In this chapter, Bible quotations are taken from the ESV.

The previous five chapters of Leviticus, containing laws about a range of things from childbirth to diet, all begin with the words "The LORD spoke to Moses" or "The LORD spoke to Moses and Aaron". But when we come to Leviticus 16 and the Day of Atonement, we find that it has a more specific frame: it was "after the death of the two sons of Aaron".

Aaron's sons had died because they tried to approach God without respect and in their own way. They "offered unauthorized fire before the LORD, which he had not commanded them" (Leviticus 10 v 1). They had approached him without thinking about the problem of God's anger against them as sinners. And so "fire came out from before the LORD and consumed them, and they died" (v 2).

We are reminded of this event at the beginning of the instructions for the Day of Atonement in order to underline the issue—the big problem which Leviticus 16 is going to solve. God is angry at sin.

And this is a problem we must take seriously. The reference to the death of Aaron's sons in 16 v 1 is like a warning: you cannot stand in the presence of God. Verse 2 makes it clear that even without committing a great, obvious offence against God as his sons did, Aaron cannot enter the presence of God either. He too is a sinner and he too would be consumed by fire if he did so. Even the high priest of Israel cannot come before the God of Israel, and live.

BUT THERE IS A WAY

Verse 3 begins...

But in this way Aaron shall come into the Holy Place.

There is a way, after all, for Aaron to enter the presence of God. And that would have been a matter of huge relief for the people of Israel.

There are two goats in Leviticus 16, which are the substitutes for Israel. They stand for the Israelites and take their place as sinners. They also therefore take the penalty, the judgment, the condemnation that Israel deserves. God's anger against sin is to be poured out on the goats instead of on Israel, so that Israel can be forgiven.

SWAP ONE: THE SIN OFFERING

What happens is that an animal is killed and its blood sprinkled on the mercy seat, the place of God's presence. Aaron does this first on his own behalf, and then for the people:

Aaron shall present the bull as a sin offering for himself, and shall make atonement for himself and for his house. He shall kill the bull as a sin offering for himself ... And he shall take some of the blood of the bull and sprinkle it with his finger on the front of the mercy seat on the east side, and in front of the mercy seat he shall sprinkle some of the blood with his finger seven times.

Then he shall kill the goat of the sin offering that is for the people and bring its blood inside the veil and do with its blood as he did with the blood of the bull, sprinkling it over the mercy seat and in front of the mercy seat. Thus he shall make atonement for the Holy Place, because of the uncleannesses of the people of Israel and because of their transgressions, all their sins.

(Leviticus 16 v 11, 14-16)

This blood is offered in all the places where the Israelites interact with God: not only the Holy Place (v 15) but also the tent of meeting (v 16) and the altar (v 18-19). Only when Aaron has this blood can he enter the presence of God.

The animals will die in the same way that Aaron's sons did. Ever since the Garden of Eden, God's anger at sin has resulted in death for sinners (Genesis 3 v 19). But here, mercifully, the animals take the place of Israel and die in their stead. God accepts their death instead of the priest's or the people's. The blood is sprinkled as an offering, and Israel can gain forgiveness.

So at the mercy seat, "propitiation" could be made—that is, God's anger with sin could be appeased so that sinners could be forgiven and come into his presence. ("Mercy seat" is also translated "place of propitiation".)

Does this start to sound familiar? It is exactly what Jesus did on the cross: he was a sacrifice for the sin of others. This is why the New Testament speaks repeatedly about Jesus' blood, which was "poured out for many for the forgiveness of sins" (Matthew 26 v 28).

The wonderful truth at the heart of the book of Leviticus—and the wonderful truth at the heart of the cross—is that God himself wants to bridge the gap between people and himself. The ceremonies outlined in Leviticus 16 and fulfilled at the cross are not invented by humans in a desperate attempt to get God to forgive them: they are given by God himself. The first step is his.

SWAP TWO: THE SCAPEGOAT

The second goat is also a substitute, but in a different way:

Aaron shall lay both his hands on the head of the live goat, and confess over it all the iniquities of the people of Israel, and all their transgressions, all their sins. And he shall put them on the head of the goat and send it away into the wilderness by the hand of a man who is in readiness. The goat shall bear all their iniquities on itself to a remote area, and he shall let the goat go free in the wilderness.
(Leviticus 16 v 21-22)

This goat, the scapegoat, takes the sin away from the presence of God and away from the camp of Israel. Now all of it is gone: "all the iniquities of the people of Israel, and all their transgressions, all their sins."

God's anger against sin meant that Adam and Eve were exiled from God's presence in Eden. In addition to death, exile continued to be a punishment for sin. But here, as with the first swap, the scapegoat takes this punishment so that Israel can remain in God's holy presence.

Imagine being Aaron, as he lays his hands on this goat and confesses all of that sin so that now the goat bears it instead of him or the people. Think what it would have been like to literally watch the greatest problem you've ever had just walk away. He watched all that sin disappear off into the wilderness. No matter what they'd done, in one day, it was just gone. All the lies, all the selfishness, everything. Gone.

For on this day shall atonement be made for you to cleanse you. You shall be clean before the LORD from all your sins.
(Leviticus 16 v 30)

God provided these two substitutes, one to be killed to avert God's wrath and the other to bear the sin away. Now the Israelites wouldn't have to bear the consequence of their own sin. Through these substitutes, God was propitiated: that is, his anger was satisfied, and they could find forgiveness.

UNCOMFORTABLE AND WEIRD

This is uncomfortable, and it is weird. It's uncomfortable to think that God's anger at us needs to be appeased. And secondly, it's weird that it could be solved with two goats.

But the cross makes no sense if God is not angry at our sin. We're far more used to the idea of a loving God than an angry one, but the God who is angry at sin is also the same God who is our loving heavenly Father. So in order to understand the cross, which joins the dots between those two aspects of God's character, we need to start by understanding and accepting God's anger at sin. That anger is driven by his love of goodness and justice. The God of the Bible is not indifferent to evil and sin. He hates it and he is justly angry about it.

Reading Leviticus 16 helps us to put ourselves in the shoes of the Israelites, and it *should* make us uncomfortable. All these ceremonies, all this slaughtering and sprinkling and offering, reminded them that their sin deserved the very worst punishment. The cross tells us the same thing about our sin.

This is what makes the gospel such good, good news. God does not primarily save us from the brokenness of the world; he primarily saves us from himself. He is angry and he cannot abide sin, and yet in his grace he provides a substitute.

But still, how could the death of that first goat be the propitiation for Israel's sins, the means by which God's anger was turned away? Answer: it couldn't. The goats were always going to be superseded.

The writer to the Hebrews makes this clear:

Since the law has but a shadow of the good things to come instead of the true form of these realities, it can never, by the same sacrifices that are continually offered every year, make perfect those who draw near ... But in these sacrifices there is a reminder of sins every year. For it is impossible for the blood of bulls and goats to take away sins.

(Hebrews 10 v 1, 3-4)

It *is* weird that a pair of goats should take away the sins of a whole people group. In fact, for all the gravity and care of the yearly ceremony, sin was never really taken away by it. The people were still sinners and still under God's wrath. And it's obvious why that's true: because the life of an animal is not equal to the life of a human being.

I am not an animal-lover. Before we got married, my wife wanted me to agree that we would have a pet. I agreed, but I made a condition: we could get a pet as long as we agreed never to refer to that pet as if it was a family member. Why? Because I was determined that we would remember this: *a pet is not a person.*

Even if you do love animals—even if you are the proud owner of the most well-behaved, friendly, or immaculate dog in the park—you will (I hope) accept that the life of an animal is not equivalent to the life of a human. If you had to choose between your wonderful pet and a family member, you would (I hope) always choose the family member. But if an animal's life is not equivalent to a human life, then there's no way that an animal could really swap with a human being—let alone a whole nation of human beings—when it came to sin. If God's anger against sin was to be dealt with properly, it would take more than the blood of a goat.

So what was the point of the Day of Atonement—of the goats and the blood? Was it all pointless? No. The Day of Atonement pointed forward to the cross, which really did deal with the anger of God, and solve the problem of all sin—past, present and future. The people of Israel were forgiven not because the substitution of two goats was in itself effective, but because they had faith in the God who promised to forgive them. The goats pointed forwards to the once-and-for-all propitiation for sins—the cross of Jesus Christ.

THE GREATEST SWAP OF ALL

The book of Hebrews explains how the Day of Atonement points to the cross:

> *Therefore, brothers, since we have confidence to enter the holy places by the blood of Jesus, by the new and living way that he opened for us through the curtain, that is, through his flesh, and since we have a great priest over the house of God, let us draw near with a true heart in full assurance of faith, with our hearts sprinkled clean from an evil conscience and our bodies washed with pure water.*
> (Hebrews 10 v 19-22)

Previously, the place of propitiation, where God's presence was, had to be sprinkled with blood. Now it is our hearts which have been metaphorically sprinkled clean—and so it is there that God's presence dwells. Previously only the priest could enter the Holy Place, and then only once a year. Now all Christians can have confidence to enter, by the blood of Christ and because of his broken body. His "flesh" is compared to the curtain which divided the Holy Place from the rest of the temple—it is through Jesus that we enter God's presence.

We can draw near in faith, because it is on the cross that God's anger against sin is dealt with. The great news of the gospel is that God sent his Son to become our propitiation— to die on the cross to take the punishment for sin.

Jesus is the fulfilment of both of the goats described in Leviticus 16. He not only shed the blood that we deserve to shed and died the death that we deserved to die; he also bore our sin away like the scapegoat, experiencing the feeling of separation from the Father. That is why he cried out from the cross, "My God, my God, why have you forsaken me?" For the first time in all of eternity, the Son of God knew something of what it felt like to be apart from the Father, experiencing hell in our place.

Jesus' blood is the blood of the eternal Son of God, and therefore it has infinite and eternal value. Because he's the Son of God, he is uniquely able to take the full wrath of God in our place. Unlike the atonement sacrifices which had to be carried out year after year, Jesus' one sacrifice was good enough for us all, for ever. He brings total and lasting forgiveness.

And so, although it may seem as though the New Testament God is about love while the Old Testament God is about anger, in fact it is in the comparison between the Day of Atonement and the cross that we find out the truth. The Day of Atonement displays the love of God in making a way for his people to come to him despite his anger at the sin which should have been relationship-ruining. In the same way, the cross of Jesus Christ is the fullest expression of the love of God precisely because it is the place where God's anger against sin is finally appeased. God's anger against us as sinners is real and serious, yet the Father determined to pour that anger onto his own Son in our place—and the Son determined to offer himself as the sacrifice for our sins. Realising that, we come to understand the wonderful and deeply generous nature of God's overwhelming love for us.

The result? Sinners are able to draw near to him eternally. As forgiven people, we have access to the very presence of God.

MAKE YOUR APPROACH

The writer to the Hebrews calls us to take this opportunity and to live in the light of Christ's sacrifice. The first thing we must do is to put our faith in Christ:

> *Let us draw near with a true heart in full assurance of faith.*
> *(Hebrews 10 v 22)*

Access to God is something we can only have because of Jesus. That means that nothing—no knowledge, no moral living, no rituals, no church attendance—guarantees you access to God, except faith in Jesus. If there were another way for us to dwell with God in peace, then Jesus would never have gone to the cross. When he prayed for the cup of God's wrath to be taken away from him, it could have been. But it was not taken away, because there was no other way to propitiate God's anger against sin and win forgiveness and acceptance for sinners.

Remember, God in his anger is like a consuming fire. If you're into nature shows, you may have seen what a forest fire looks like. It's absolutely devastating. A forest fire destroys everything in its path. It consumes everything. It's a scary and serious thing to be in a forest when a fire starts.

And yet I have it on good authority that there is a place, even in a forest fire, where it's possible to be safe. Once the fire has gone through a certain part of a forest, it has burned absolutely everything that can be burned, and will never come back there again. So the safe place to be in a forest fire is a place where the fire has already burned.

The Bible tells us that one day things will come to an end and Jesus will return in judgment. It's going to be like a fire, and it's going to be far greater than any forest fire. It will sweep through everything. There will be no escape, no corner of the earth that is somehow left untouched. If you are guilty of sin—and all of us are—then the fire of God's judgment is an incredibly scary place to be. But there is a safe place: one safe place. That is to be found in Jesus Christ, who has already undergone the fire of God's anger.

If we confess our sins to Jesus and trust in him then all the anger that we deserve has already been poured out on him. Jesus has undergone the fire of God's anger, and so he is a safe place for us. He is the one place to run to.

God withholds the full extent of his anger now in order to give us the maximum opportunity to run to Jesus and have our sin dealt with before the judgment day. But when that day comes, there will be no more chances. So I don't want to take it for granted that just because you're reading this book, you are trusting in Jesus Christ. If you are not, take the opportunity now to trust in him. Trust in the God who, because he loves you, has made a way for you to find full forgiveness from everything you have ever done wrong. Trust in the Son, who willingly made himself a sacrifice for sin and who suffered and died that you might live.

Trusting in him means you can approach God without fear. You have been forgiven. You have been made holy. You can go boldly into the Holy Place, "in full assurance of faith". You can now enjoy life with God.

HOLD ON TO YOUR HOPE

For those of us who are trusting in Christ for forgiveness and salvation, there is a second instruction:

> Let us hold fast the confession of our hope without wavering, for he who promised is faithful.
>
> (Hebrews 10 v 23)

Have you ever thought in the back of your head that God is angry with you? Many of us have. We have this sense that God is out to get us and to punish us. We want to go to God in prayer, but we have this sense that God doesn't want us to go to him. Or perhaps we wake up on Sunday morning and we get ready for church, but then we think about the way we've lived our lives over the past week, and question whether God really wants us there.

It is at times like these that we need to remember the scapegoat on the Day of Atonement. Remember Aaron, watching the sin walk away into the wilderness? Jesus is your scapegoat, and so your sin has been taken away. The cross should remind us that God is no longer angry with us. He has forgiven us. We are no longer enemies, but friends of God. We are children of God. There is no more anger left for those who are trusting in Jesus, because he has drunk to the very bottom the cup of God's wrath for us. So we can go confidently before God, knowing that the arms of the Father are always open wide to us and are always inviting us into his presence. "He who promised is faithful."

We shouldn't be alone as we hold fast to this hope that we have. We do it together.

And let us consider how to stir up one another to love and good works, not neglecting to meet together, as is the habit of some, but encouraging one another, and all the more as you see the Day drawing near.
(Hebrews 10 v 24-25)

You need others to remind you: *Jesus is the propitiation for your sins. God cannot be angry with you. God is only ever for you. You are forgiven.* And you need to remind others of these truths, too.

This is all the more important as we "see the Day drawing near". Just as the access the Israelites had to God was a mere shadow of the access that we have gained to him in Christ, so our access to God's presence now is a shadow compared to what it will be like on that final day. After judgment comes the new creation. On this side of things we approach God in prayer, but there will come a day when we'll be with God in all his awesome fullness. Not only will there be forgiveness—there will actually be no further need for forgiveness, because we'll be perfect. We will dwell with God as forgiven people for ever.

That is the ultimate hope that we have in the cross, and it is a hope that should transform the way we live now. Jesus has not just drawn God's anger away from us, he has not just removed our sin, but he has secured us an eternal home with God. And we will worship him there. We will sing for all eternity of how God, through the death of his Son upon the cross, provided a propitiation for his own anger against sin. Forgiveness was won and we can enjoy dwelling for ever in his full, perfect, life-giving presence.

QUESTIONS FOR DISCUSSION

1. What is your experience of how sin affects your relationships with others?

2. How would you explain why God is angry at sin?

3. Imagine you were an Israelite at the first Day of Atonement. How do you think you would have felt?

4. What do you find strange or uncomfortable about these rituals?

5. Why is it important and a good thing that God takes sin seriously?

6. How many links between the Day of Atonement and the cross can you spot in Hebrews 10 v 19-22?

7. How does the cross give you confidence today? How does it change the way you look at the future?

8. Who could you remind of the truth of God's forgiveness in the coming week?

THE STORY CONTINUES

The Israelites had been a nation for hundreds of years by the time the book of Isaiah was written. Their history had seen sin after sin. The books of Judges, Samuel, Kings and Chronicles tell countless stories of injustice and crime. God's people knew well the problem of sin and the judgment they deserved for it. They were now facing the threat of annihilation by surrounding nations whom God was using to exact punishment.

But in Isaiah 53 there is a prophecy which looks forward to the time when punishment for sin would end: when God's justice would be satisfied and sin would be defeated. It speaks about a servant who would take the punishment of the guilty.

In Acts 8, after Jesus had died, risen and ascended to heaven, Philip met an Ethiopian eunuch who was reading Isaiah 53:

> *The eunuch said to Philip, "About whom, I ask you, does the prophet say this, about himself or about someone else?" Then Philip opened his mouth, and beginning with this Scripture he told him the good news about Jesus.*
>
> *(Acts 8 v 34-35)*

Philip revealed what Isaiah 53 was really about. This chapter, written hundreds of years before Jesus was born, is a prophecy about the cross.

3. JUSTICE

HOW GOD JUSTIFIES THE GUILTY
KEVIN DEYOUNG

We tend to repackage the word "sin," because we know instinctively that people find the idea, and even the word itself, offensive.[4] Everyone knows that the world is not as it's supposed to be, and I've never met anyone who told me they're perfect. But we have all sorts of euphemisms for speaking of sin, so that we can feel that it is not really our problem. We write it off as mere biological misfiring or we blame it on our education or on our parents. We say it's just a "growth edge" or a "learning curve." We try to shift the blame.

Perhaps that is why the current president of the USA has said that he has had no reason to repent of sin. It isn't something that we think of as *our* problem.

---

[4] Some of the material in this chapter was also covered in my chapter "Justification for Today" in Scott M. Manetsch, *The Reformation and the Irrepressible Word of God* (IVP US 2019).

The previous president, meanwhile, when asked to define sin, said that it is whatever is out of line with his own values. In that way of speaking, sin *is* our problem. It is a personal failing, a reason to be disappointed with oneself. But it is not really a *serious* problem, because it's based on our own personal feelings of right and wrong, and those can change.

But in fact, as we saw in the last chapter, sin is what is out of line with God and his word. It is something for which each one of us is deeply responsible. And it cannot be written off as just a violation of our own personal values. To sin is to commit a deep injustice against God.

David, the most important of Israel's kings and the writer of many psalms, is a good example of this. He sinned against Bathsheba, in using his power to make her sleep with him; he sinned against Joab, in using his power to make him have a man killed; he sinned against Uriah the Hittite, who *was* the man killed; and he sinned against his people, in not leading them well. There was almost no one that he did not sin against. And yet he said to God in Psalm 51 v 4, "Against you, you only, have I sinned," because ultimately all of that horizontal sin—all that wrongdoing against other people— also had a vertical dimension.[5] It was an affront and an offense to a holy God. When we sin, we are not just out of line with our own values, but with God's. We fall short of God's righteousness. We are guilty of breaking his holy law.

And when you break the law, you deserve punishment. Judgment has to happen, and it has to happen not only

[5] In this chapter, Bible quotations are taken from the ESV.

because God is angry with sin but also simply because he is just.

Paul emphasizes this in Romans 3 v 5-6:

What shall we say? That God is unrighteous to inflict wrath on us? (I speak in a human way.) By no means! For then how could God judge the world?

God has to judge the world—he has to judge sinners—in order to make things right. Maybe the reason some of us don't feel the weight of sin and the necessity of judgment is because of how little we have really suffered at the hands of ungodliness. When you've seen real ungodliness, real injustice—and I don't mean when somebody swerves in front of you when you're driving, or when you have to wait a long time for customer service; I mean real, profound injustice—then everything in you screams out: *This is not right.* When someone commits a terrible crime, we want justice. We want judgment. We do not want that person to go free.

Yet here is the tension: somehow, we manage to care deeply about justice being served on other people, and at the same time brush off our own wrongdoing as if it doesn't really matter or isn't really our fault. This is inconsistent. We have all done things that are unjust.

So God's judgment is a good thing. Christ will one day come in judgment and make the world right. But at the same time, God's judgment is also a terrifying thing, because we are sinners.

And yet Paul tells us that we are justified—declared completely innocent—in Christ. Though criminals, we experience no punishment because Jesus took it on himself instead:

All have sinned and fall short of the glory of God, and are justified by his grace as a gift, through the redemption that is in Christ Jesus, whom God put forward as a propitiation by his blood, to be received by faith.
(Romans 3 v 23-25)

But how can this be right? How can this be the action of a righteous and just God—to let sinners go free and to punish the innocent?

This is the tension that we find in Isaiah 53.

HOW CAN THIS BE?

The prophecy actually begins at the end of chapter 52, in verse 13. There, in some translations, a heading is added: "He was pierced for our transgressions." This chapter is going to tell us that this righteous person, this sinless servant, suffers for the crimes of the wicked.

53 v 1 acknowledges that this seems like an injustice:

Who has believed what he has heard from us?

This message about the suffering servant is scarcely to be believed. How can it be that one so righteous should be so brutally punished? And this problem only builds as the chapter goes on.

Isaiah describes sin again and again, and the language sounds harsh to our ears. He speaks of "transgression" in verses 5 and 8 and "transgressors" in verse 12; of "iniquities" three times (v 5, 6, 11); of how sinners are "wicked" (v 9); and of "guilt" (v 10). He speaks of "oppression" in verse 8—not oppression that we suffer, but oppression that we inflict. All these words are descriptions of us and of our actions. God's people, people like us, are depicted as selfish, lawless, foolish sinners. The picture is not a flattering one. This is our sin, and our guilt.

Meanwhile, verse 9 tells us this servant "had done no violence, and there was no deceit in his mouth." No deceit. Good people may have suffered before—Job, for example—but Isaiah is saying something more. This suffering servant had done *nothing* wrong. No violence: not in his heart, not in his actions, not ever. No deceitful words; no lustful thoughts. No sin whatsoever. This is what makes his suffering so unbelievable. It seems so unjust. It is a punishment for things he has not done. It is a punishment for things *we* have done:

> ... he was pierced for our transgressions;
> he was crushed for our iniquities ...
> and the LORD has laid on him
> the iniquity of us all. *(Isaiah 53 v 5a, 6b)*

The torrent of anguish upon the servant keeps building and building. "His appearance was ... marred, beyond human semblance" (52 v 14). He was "despised and rejected" (53 v 3). He was stricken, smitten, and afflicted (v 4); pierced, crushed, wounded, oppressed, cut off, killed, and buried.

> *And they made his grave with the wicked ...*
> *although he had done no violence,*
> *and there was no deceit in his mouth.*   *(Isaiah 53 v 9)*

How can this be: that one so righteous would be so brutally punished, and punished in place of the guilty?

Is it a mistake—some cruel accident, some profound misfortune? After all, God's people suffer all the time. They face injustice, are wrongly accused, have to put up with terrible things. Is this just one of those sad, twisted tales; a case of man's inhumanity toward man?

No, something deeper is going on. This suffering servant is God's own Son.

GOD'S DELIBERATE PLAN

The first thing we need to understand about the suffering of Jesus is that it was part of an eternal plan, made between the members of the Trinity. It was no accident.

The servant in Isaiah 53 suffers willingly. He *voluntarily* takes the punishment of the wicked. And therefore he endures the affliction silently:

> *He was oppressed, and he was afflicted,*
> *yet he opened not his mouth;*
> *like a lamb that is led to the slaughter,*
> *and like a sheep that before its shearers is silent,*
> *so he opened not his mouth.*   *(Isaiah 53 v 7)*

In the previous verse, sinners too are compared to sheep:

All we like sheep have gone astray;
we have turned—every one—to his own way.

(Isaiah 53 v 6a)

We are supposed to notice the contrast here. Sinners are like sheep in that we wander and go astray. But the servant is like a sheep in that he approaches his slaughter without a word. He does not go astray but knowingly embraces what has been determined for him.

Do not picture the Lord Jesus going to his death kicking and flailing and bemoaning his fate. In John 10 v 18 Jesus said that no one would take his life away: he would lay it down of his own accord. Yes, he asked the Father to remove this cup of suffering from him; but he also said, "Not my will, but yours, be done" (Luke 22 v 42). We must not think that the Father punished the Son as a hapless victim of some cosmic child abuse. No, the Son went to the cross freely, willingly.

More importantly still, this was not simply Jesus' own plan, but one which he conceived together with the Father:

It was the will of the LORD to crush him;
he has put him to grief.   *(Isaiah 53 v 10)*

This righteous servant suffered on our behalf because it was God's will. This is the very heart of our good news. Because it was the Lord's will to crush him, and no accident, we can behold the glory of our triune God in planning and procuring our salvation. The Son is not a divine good cop, appeasing a divine bad cop. He and the Father planned it together.

The Father sent the Son, and the Son, in union of purpose with the Father and the Holy Spirit, agreed to be the agent of this salvation plan. On the cross Jesus did experience a kind of God-forsakenness, but that does not indicate any rift in the eternal internal dynamics of the Trinity. They were always at one.

Nor is it the case that Jesus' death changed God's mind about sinners. It is not that God hated us at first, and only after the cross did he begin to love us. Good Friday happened because God already loved those whom he had chosen in Christ. He had already set his affections upon us, already planned to make us his treasured possessions:

For God so loved the world, that he gave his only Son.
(John 3 v 16)

In this is love, not that we have loved God but that he loved us and sent his Son to be the propitiation for our sins.
(1 John 4 v 10)

Don't think that God's love is just a result of the cross. God's love is what led to the cross.

Moreover, the fact that it was the Lord's will to crush his servant means that we can have full confidence in the cross: we can be certain that Jesus really did take the punishment for our sin.

If it had not been God's will, then he would have been able to say, *Well, that wasn't my doing. I didn't sign up to this deal. I'm not sure that that really is enough.* But since it was God's plan from all eternity, then we can be confident of his intentions. This was the eternal agreement between the Father and the Son. This is how they were always going to solve the problem of sin. Jesus died "according to the definite plan and foreknowledge of God" (Acts 2 v 23).

So this is the good news: that the Father did not spare his own Son, but gave him up for us all, and that the Son willingly drank the bitter cup of God's wrath for our sakes.

It was no random injustice. It was the plan of the triune God all along.

FULLY, FINALLY, FOREVER

Jesus' suffering and death on the cross means that the punishment required by sin has been paid. In this sense, justice has been satisfied. But a question remains. It is the question that we started with. How can this swap be an expression of justice? Jesus went willingly, yes. The Father sent him, yes. But how is it fair that Jesus should suffer on our behalf? How can God be just in condemning the righteous and setting free the ungodly?

In the course of his great explanation of justification in Romans 3 – 4, Paul says something that may seem curious to us:

Jesus our Lord ... was delivered up for our trespasses and raised for our justification. (Romans 4 v 24-25)

We tend to think that the *cross* is about justification. So why does Paul say here that Jesus was *raised* for our justification? What is the connection between the tomb being empty and you and I being justified?

The resurrection declares something about Jesus' work on the cross. It tells us that justice has been satisfied, and that sinners who belong to Christ have been justified. It tells us for certain that all our sins have been fully paid for.

Think of it this way.

I have eight kids. Suppose that, one weekend, the eldest is being very good and doing his homework. But the other seven don't want to do their homework. They're bored. Mom and Dad aren't around—or they don't think we're around. So they're wandering around the house, looking for something to cause mischief with. Then one of them finds some fireworks, the fireworks that we've put away ready for Thanksgiving and that the kids are not supposed to know about. Soon they're all in the garden exploding things: sending rockets into the sky, lighting fuse after fuse, blowing it all up.

But suppose Mom and Dad—my wife and I—are actually in the house after all. We come out and we confront the seven children who have participated in this crime. And when they see us, all seven of them are absolutely terrified. But just as the younger siblings are about to get what is their due, just as we are about to go ballistic, the eldest brother comes outside too. He steps forward, and even though he had no part in his siblings' actions, he offers to be punished in their place. And so we send him to his room: *You are going to stay there, you are not going to have supper, and you are not going to come out until we tell you to.*

As long as the older brother is up in his room, the seven wayward children are a bit nervous. *Is this actually going to work? Are Mom and Dad serious about this?* As long as the room is occupied, they are not confident that parental justice has been satisfied. But as soon as the door opens and big brother comes out, and we tell him he is free to go, that empty room indicates the satisfaction of parental justice. It *did* work. The debt has been paid for. The guilt has been cleared. The punishment has been completed.[6]

You see the connection. The empty tomb on Easter morning is a sign that the swap has worked. The punishment for sin is death, so if Jesus defeats death, then he must have taken all the punishment. There is none left. The resurrection is the loud declaration that the swap has worked, justice is satisfied, and there is nothing left to pay.

Peter explains this in Acts 2 v 24:

God raised him up, loosing the pangs of death, because it was not possible for him to be held by it.

---

[6] I used a similar illustration in my book *The Good News We Almost Forgot* (Moody 2010), pages 92-93.

Jesus could not possibly stay dead. The grave could not hold the Son of God because it had no claim on him. When a sin is paid for, there is no obligation to pay any further penalty for that sin. And so the resurrection proves that sin is indeed fully paid for. Jesus, even after bearing our sin, is righteous: he cannot continue to be punished. The punishment is over. Therefore, those who trust in Christ are saved. Our sins are fully and finally and forever forgiven.

FORGIVENESS IS JUST

What this shows us, too, is that we are saved not by the removal of justice but by the satisfaction of justice.

It would be a mistake to think that we're saved because God one day just said, *You know what? Your sin? Forget about it. It's no big deal.* That is not how justification— being found utterly innocent in God's sight—works. We are not justified because God's mercy obliterated God's justice. We are justified because in divine mercy, God sent his Son to satisfy divine justice by paying the penalty for sin.

God would not be God if he did not act according to his righteousness. It would be a denial of who he is. The way a just God can justify the ungodly is not by setting aside justice but by satisfying it:

> *[Jesus' death] was to show [God's] righteousness at the present time, so that he might be just and the justifier of the one who has faith in Jesus.* (Romans 3 v 26)

The result is that now, if you belong to Christ, you can have total confidence that there is no punishment left for you. It would go against God's name and his character if your sins were not forgiven. It is an expression of God's justice that you are saved. You are free of punishment because Jesus has already been punished on your behalf, and it would be unjust for you to be punished again.

That is why the apostle John was able to write:

> If we confess our sins, he is faithful and just to forgive us our sins and to cleanse us from all unrighteousness.
> (1 John 1 v 9b)

Wouldn't you expect it to say that he's faithful and *loving*, or that he's faithful and *merciful*, or that he's faithful and *gracious*, and that's why he forgives us? Those things are true, but here, John chooses to say that he is faithful and *just*. His justice is the reason why he forgives and cleanses us. He can do so because he himself has satisfied the demands of justice.

SWAPPING RIGHTEOUSNESS

But there is even more good news. Because Christ fulfilled all the requirements of the law, he is able not only to fully pay the penalty for my sin but also to give me his own righteousness. I become like him: "his offspring" (Isaiah 53 v 10). One of the most wonderful things about the cross is that by it I do not just avoid punishment for my guilt—I actually become guiltless in God's sight.

Isaiah 53 continues...

> *Out of the anguish of his soul he shall see and be satisfied;*
> *by his knowledge shall the righteous one, my servant,*
> *make many to be accounted righteous,*
> *and he shall bear their iniquities.* (v 11)

This language, being "accounted righteous," is also used by Paul in Romans 3 – 4. He compares us to Abraham, who "believed God, and it was counted to him as righteousness" (4 v 3). Likewise...

> *To the one who ... believes in him who justifies the ungodly,*
> *his faith is counted as righteousness.* (Romans 4 v 5)

Christ bore the curse of the law so that in him we become the righteousness of God. The theological language is that his righteousness is "imputed" to us. That means it is credited to our account. It's the difference between holding a banknote which belongs to someone else and having them wire the same amount to your bank account, credited to belong to you. You have Christ's righteousness not merely as an example to follow, but as something which is your very own. Christ does not only take away the punishment you deserve; he also gives you his own righteousness, and his own innocence. You swap your unrighteousness for his righteousness. This is the gift, and the great exchange, for all who believe in him.

Here's how Charles Hodge, a 19th-century theologian, put it in his *Exposition of the Second Epistle to the Corinthians*:

"Our sins were the judicial ground of the sufferings of Christ so that they were a satisfaction of justice. His righteousness is the judicial ground of our acceptance with God, so that our pardon is an act of justice." (page 151)

This is why God shows justice in forgiving us. We have been made righteous, guiltless, by the cross. And so we see that justice is shot through the entire plan of salvation. People go to hell because God is just, and people go to heaven because God is just. Because our sins were counted to Christ, he deserved to die; and because his life and death are counted to us, we deserve to live. In all respects God's justice is satisfied.

THE HIGHEST EXPRESSION OF JUSTICE

I believe many of us have barely begun to grasp how good this good news is, how secure our salvation is, and how completely and unalterably justified we are through faith in Christ. God did not set aside the law in sending Jesus to the cross. He fulfilled the law.

If you are in Christ, you are not justified because God waved a magic wand and decided to overlook your faults. No, he has not overlooked the tiniest speck of any one of your faults. He demands justice for every one of your iniquities and every one of your transgressions.

If you ever think to yourself, *What I deserve for all the things that I have done is condemnation, punishment, shame,* then you're right. Sin deserves punishment. God demands justice for every lustful look, every proud thought, every spiteful word. He will not overlook any of it, because he is perfectly just. But the death and resurrection of the crucified Son of God tell us that all the demands of justice have already been met. Everyone who belongs to Christ has had all of their guilt really and truly and forever forgiven; instead they become sinless and innocent in God's sight.

The cross is not a story about how to endure suffering or how to help others who suffer. It is not just a story about a good man who died a sad death. The cross is about the punishment for sins, and the resurrection is the loud declaration that Jesus is enough. He is enough to atone for every wrong thing you will ever do; enough to reconcile you to God; enough to present you holy in God's presence; enough to free you from the curse of judgment; enough to assure you that there is no condemnation for you; enough to finally and fully set you free from the penalty and ultimately from the power of sin.

If we are in Christ, it will be counted to us as righteousness when we believe in him who raised from the dead Jesus, our Lord: delivered up for our trespasses, raised for our justification. Praise God for the cross.

QUESTIONS FOR DISCUSSION

1. Why might the idea that we are all sinners seem offensive?

2. Why is it important to remember that the cross was the deliberate plan of God—both Father and Son?

3. Why is it important that Jesus was raised to life?

4. What does it mean that Jesus' righteousness is "imputed" to us?

5. How would you answer someone who says that the cross was unjust?

6. How would you explain the cross to someone who feels consumed by guilt?

7. How would you explain the cross to someone who says that they have done nothing wrong?

THE STORY CONTINUES

Several hundred years after Isaiah's prophecy, Christ came. The Gospel narratives tell us how he performed miracles to announce his identity, gathered followers, and taught them about God.

By chapter 8 of Mark's Gospel, Peter is convinced of who Jesus is. "You are the Messiah" (v 29). He knows that Jesus is God's anointed King, who has come to take away the sins of the world. But Peter still hasn't understood how Jesus is going to do that.

So Jesus next teaches his disciples that he must suffer and die. And this will not only save them; it will also give them an entirely new purpose for living.

4. PURPOSE

HOW THE CROSS CALLS US TO MISSION
RICHARD COEKIN

The Royal National Lifeboat Institution (RNLI) has a fleet of 444 lifeboats operating from 238 stations along the coastline of Britain, offering a magnificent round-the-clock search and rescue service. Most of the RNLI lifeboat crews are volunteers, inspired by the call of RNLI founder, Sir William Hillary—who himself took part in many rescues—to "risk their own lives for those they have never known or seen". Almost entirely funded by voluntary donations, since its formation in 1824 the service is reckoned to have saved 140,000 people—but at the terrible cost of more than 600 lives.

The stated purpose of the RNLI is quite simple: "to save lives at sea".

Jesus Christ said something similar when he spoke about his own purpose in coming from heaven to die. Speaking of eternal salvation, he said:

For the Son of Man came to seek and to save the lost.
(Luke 19 v 10)[7]

So when he called some fishermen to be his first disciples, he called them to share his mission. "'Come, follow me,' Jesus said, 'and I will send you out to fish for people'" (Matthew 4 v 19). As he preached the gospel in Galilee, "When he saw the crowds, he had compassion on them, because they were harassed and helpless, like sheep without a shepherd", desperately in need of him (Matthew 9 v 36). Then he identified for his disciples the most urgent need of his mission to our world: "The harvest is plentiful but the workers are few" (v 37).

And before Jesus ascended to glory, he commissioned all his followers to be such workers in his global mission: "Go and make disciples of all nations" (Matthew 28 v 19). This must now be the primary purpose of our lives and our churches. Indeed, it is for the purpose of making disciples that our Father in heaven has delayed the end of the world and for this purpose that believers are still here and not yet in heaven. Christian churches are a lot like lifeboats. We are dedicated to saving people.

To quote from the RNLI website, "Our crews are prepared to drop everything and risk their lives to save others at a moment's notice." And Christians are to behave like these crews. Jesus did not commission his churches to be like cruise ships, full of passengers dedicated to their own comfort; nor to be like battleships, firing angry broadsides

[7] In this chapter, Bible quotations are taken from the NIV.

at each other. He wants his churches to be like lifeboats, with sacrificial volunteer crews devoted 24/7 to saving people from drowning in sin to become his disciples. This is not to diminish the importance of worshipping God, teaching Scripture or caring for one another within a church family. It is to recognise that these ministries empower God's people for the great purpose of following Jesus in saving lives—making disciples of all nations for Jesus, to the glory of God.

And having said Christian churches are like lifeboats, I'm not thinking so much of the sleek new E-class boats we now have on the River Thames in London, powered by massive Volvo engines at speeds of 40 knots. I'm thinking of all kinds of ordinary lifeboats, many of them small inflatable dinghies, manned by exhausted crews struggling to pull drowning people out of the ocean. They don't look very impressive and they certainly don't feel very powerful; but in 2018, with lifeboats such as these, at an average of 24 callouts per day, the RNLI managed to save 118 lives. In the same way, most Christians and churches look very unimpressive and feel very weak, and yet God is constantly using such ordinary, weary congregations to save people who were once drowning in sin.

Of course, salvation has already been *accomplished* by Jesus on the cross. We've seen that by his death Jesus secured our freedom from slavery to sin, forgiveness from the corruption of sin, and justification from the guilt of sin. But the salvation he accomplished must now be made known through proclamation. For it is through our evangelism that Christ calls those he has chosen and has died to save. As Paul later puts it, "And how can they believe in the one of whom they have not heard?" (Romans 10 v 14). God *accomplished* the salvation of his people on the cross, so now the gospel of Christ crucified must be *proclaimed* to all nations. This is the glorious purpose to which Jesus has called us.

But it can be costly to proclaim the cross. In the West we don't normally expect to be killed for spreading the gospel—unlike the brothers and sisters in North Korea laid down under a steamroller (documented in a 2016 report by Christian Solidarity Worldwide), or in Eritrea imprisoned in metal shipping containers to die in the desert (reported by Open Doors in 2017), or in Iran where believers are routinely arrested and even tortured. But even in Westernised cultures it can still be costly to speak of Christ crucified: costly in social rejection or family tension, costly in our careers or marital status, costly in time and money spent supporting the evangelistic activities of our churches and overseas missions. Why would we volunteer for such a challenging mission, when most people are just trying to earn enough to buy a dream property or move to a dream climate, raise a perfect family or get a perfect job?

The answer, of course, is Jesus. He is not only our loving Saviour who suffered for our sins, and our living Lord who has commanded us to make disciples; he is also the one who has explicitly called us to follow his example in suffering for the sake of others:

Whoever wants to be my disciple must deny themselves and take up their cross and follow me.   (Mark 8 v 34)

Just as the cross was the purpose of Jesus' life, he wants us to take up our own cross as the purpose of ours.

FOLLOWING IN JESUS' FOOTSTEPS

Mark records this extraordinary calling upon all our lives in his Gospel, just after it reaches its dramatic mid-point. Peter has realised who Jesus is, declaring, "You are the Messiah" (Mark 8 v 29). Now Jesus can begin to teach his purpose in coming:

He then began to teach them that the Son of Man must suffer many things and be rejected by the elders, the chief priests and the teachers of the law, and that he must be killed and after three days rise again. He spoke plainly about this.   (Mark 8 v 31-32)

Peter did not like this at all and began to rebuke Jesus. He didn't want a suffering and rejected Christ. He wanted a successful and popular leader who would call his followers to share his success and popularity. Jesus recognised in Peter both the worldliness of sin and the lies of Satan— tempting Jesus' disciples then and now to avoid his way of suffering.

Jesus could only save lives by suffering on the cross. This was the purpose of his life. This was why he called the crowd together to explain in verses 34-38 that his followers must follow him down this way of the cross. Serving others, especially by proclaiming the gospel for their salvation, even in weakness, humiliation and suffering, must be the purpose of our lives as it was the purpose of his. In these simple phrases—"deny themselves", "take up their cross", and "follow me", we hear three commands.

DENY YOURSELF: BE WILLING TO SERVE

To "deny" yourself means neglecting yourself to give others what they need—especially the good news of Christ crucified, who saves us from hell for heaven for ever.

Jesus denied himself to serve us. He left his glorious home in heaven to be born into deprivation on earth. He came as a missionary to preach the gospel. He surrendered himself to suffering for our salvation. Following him means becoming like him: denying ourselves, being willing to serve those around us, and especially by sharing the gospel whatever the cost. Jesus doesn't say, *Comfort yourself with my love,* or *Improve yourself with my power,* but *Deny yourself for my purpose.*

In our rights-oriented generation, denying ourselves for the sake of others is radical. We're constantly being encouraged to do whatever makes us happy: indulge our desires, spend on ourselves, avoid difficult people and give our children the best. But Jesus says we must deny ourselves in the service of others. One young family who moved onto a deprived housing estate in London to support a church plant were told by worldly sceptics, "That's no place to bring up children!" But Jesus was calling us *and* our children when he said, "Whoever wants to be my disciple must deny themselves".

This isn't religious asceticism—trying to impress God with pointless hardship, like the fifth-century monk Simeon Stylites, who sold all his possessions to go and live on top of a stone pillar in the Syrian desert for 37 years, resourced by his friends. The Bible makes it clear that forbidding the grateful enjoyment of God's good gifts such as marriage and food is actually demonic because it denies God's kindness (1 Timothy 4 v 1-5). Jesus wasn't a masochist. He didn't go to the cross because he liked pain. He went because it was the only way to save sinners. So, like Jesus, we can enjoy the good gifts of our Father; but we must also be willing to make costly sacrifices for the salvation of others. Jesus says that if you want to be his disciple, you must deny yourself. Your purpose is to serve others—especially for their salvation.

TAKE UP YOUR CROSS: BE WILLING TO SUFFER

Secondly, Jesus says his disciples must "take up their cross". These are hugely sobering words. Jesus compares life as a Christian to the horrifying experience of a condemned criminal, staggering along under the weight of the crossbeam to which they will soon be nailed to die in excruciating agony. Jesus knew such a death awaited him, and calls us to follow him. He is saying that we will have to carry a cross of shame in this world if we want to wear a crown of glory in the next.

Notice that he calls us to "take up" our cross: that is, to pick it up ourselves. He will not force us to do it. He calls us to volunteer to suffer the cost for the salvation of others.

During World War Two, the German pastor Dietrich Bonhoeffer was imprisoned and executed for his stand against Hitler. While in prison, he wrote some famous reflections on the Christian life, collected under the title *The Cost of Discipleship*. Among these reflections he wrote the following words:

> "When Christ calls a man, he bids him come and die. Suffering, then, is the badge of true discipleship. The disciple is not above his master. If we refuse to take up our cross and submit to suffering and rejection at the hands of men, we forfeit our fellowship with Christ and have ceased to follow him."

What is this cross we must take up? Jesus says each must "take up *their* cross" (my italics). Each follower has their own cross to bear. It will not be Jesus' cross—Jesus alone suffered for our sins, which means we will never have to endure punishment for something we've done. The Bible is clear that God does discipline his children because he loves us—so he may train and discipline us with hardship. But we will never face any of the punishment we deserve, because all of our punishment was suffered by Jesus instead of us.

And it won't be anyone else's cross either. Every follower of Jesus will be carrying their own cross in different seasons of life, so we mustn't assume that other people have it easy or feel envious of them. We can't know how heavy their cross feels or why God has given it to them. Our own cross will be the cost to us, as the people we are, in the circumstances God has designed for us, of contributing what we can to making disciples of all nations for him—knowing that Jesus wants to reward us in eternity. Jesus said:

Blessed are you when people insult you, persecute you and falsely say all kinds of evil against you because of me. Rejoice and be glad, because great is your reward in heaven.
(Matthew 5 v 11-12)

Each of us will be given the cross that our loving heavenly Father chooses for us, knowing that he works all things for our good in helping us become more like Jesus.

Of course, the blessings for such faithfulness to Jesus are not only in heaven but are also to some degree experienced now, in our local church. Jesus said:

No one who has left home or brothers or sisters or mother or father or children or fields for me and the gospel ... will fail to receive a hundred times as much in this present age: homes, brothers, sisters, mothers, children and fields—along with persecutions—and in the age to come eternal life. *(Mark 10 v 29-30)*

In our local churches we do enjoy the radically ordinary hospitality of many homes, the affectionate support of many brothers and sisters, the experienced wisdom of many mothers and fathers, the shared joys of raising many children, and the reassurance of shared material security. I shall never forget the joy of one of our church elders, without children of his own, standing in as "the father of the bride" at the wedding of an Indian girl at our church who had converted from Islam and been rejected by her family.

But we will carry a *cross*. Not the normal hardships of life, but the particular costs of proclaiming Christ crucified. If it isn't painful, it isn't a cross. For we can't become like Jesus without learning to follow God even when it hurts.

As we have seen, the costs of following Jesus are very real. Many will suffer the hurt of social rejection, family criticism or mockery at work. Some will suffer the cost of moving home to live somewhere they didn't want to live in order to support a new church plant. Others will give up well-paid jobs to train for gospel ministry. Others still will give their savings or refinance a property to pay for gospel ministries or missionaries. In some places, believers face the real possibility of imprisonment for their faith. For all of us there is the ordinary burden of turning up each week to serve at church, offering hospitality and serving in countless ways to help people of all ages and backgrounds find salvation in Jesus.

Jesus' command poses questions for all of us. What cost are you enduring in following Jesus? What cost could you pick up to help more people find salvation? Why not pray and ask your pastor if there is something you could do to help save the lost? And if you can already see your particular cross in front of you, Jesus says, "Take up your cross". Pick it up and be ready to suffer in making disciples of all nations for Jesus.

FOLLOW JESUS: INVEST IN ETERNITY

Thirdly, and lastly, Jesus simply says, "follow me". Follow Jesus. This means being willing to learn. If we're following Jesus along this way of the cross, he will lead us by his Spirit through his word—constantly encouraging, strengthening and training us. He also puts us in churches where we can encourage and spur one another on. We will never be alone if we walk this way of the cross.

In the following verses of Mark 8, as we consider the cost of his purpose for our lives, Jesus encourages us with some exciting truths about our eternity with him. He illustrates the long-term benefits of denying ourselves and taking up our cross to follow him with some simple commercial principles.

First, in verse 35, Jesus gets us to think about savings:

> For whoever wants to save their life will lose it, but whoever loses their life for me and for the gospel will save it.

We all recognise the wisdom of putting money away to save for the future: for a home, for a wedding or for our retirement. Jesus says that if we try to keep our lives for ourselves, we'll lose our lives with God. But if we surrender our lives to his purpose of saving others, even if some suggest we're throwing our lives away, in fact God will give us life with him for ever. Giving our life to him is like putting it in a savings account for the future.

Second, in verse 36, Jesus urges us to think about investments:

What good is it for someone to gain the whole world, yet forfeit their soul?

We all recognise the wisdom of investing wisely—perhaps in a house that grows in value. But there's no point investing our lives in becoming billionaires for our short time on this earth, if we have nothing of value for God to reward in eternity. Better to invest wisely in our eternal future by serving God's evangelistic mission now. Better to be more interested in trying out our church international outreach than trying out the latest sushi restaurant. Better to be more concerned to invest in our children's spiritual education than their sports education. This requires thinking long-term: investing in God's kingdom of heaven rather than our own little kingdoms on earth.

Third, in verse 37 Jesus prompts us to think about currency:

Or what can anyone give in exchange for their soul?

We all recognise the wisdom of having the right currency if we travel abroad. A huge wad of £50 notes is useless in France. A pile of dollar bills will not get you very far in Germany. Likewise, the currency that works in heaven is not the success or wealth or popularity that work on earth.

They will get you nothing. And we certainly can't buy an eternity for our souls with material things. In truth only Jesus can save our souls. His death alone has purchased our freedom, forgiveness and justification. So the only currency worth anything in heaven is following Jesus. Better by far to live by faith in Christ crucified, following his way of the cross in costly mission.

For example, I think of young people spending their evenings knocking on doors to invite people to church; of a young woman who leads a Christian ministry in her office being required to undergo "diversity training" because her bosses disapprove of her loyalty to the Bible; of a young man who has gone to live in the Middle East to reach Muslims with the good news of Jesus; of a couple who recently gave up their jobs in the city of London to go to the Gambia to help build up a Bible training school; of a businessman who visits a prison to lead Bible studies. They know that the only currency of any value in heaven is living sacrificially to help make disciples of all nations for Jesus.

Finally, in verse 38, Jesus calls us to think about loyalty:

If anyone is ashamed of me and of my words in this adulterous and sinful generation, the Son of Man will be ashamed of them when he comes in his Father's glory with the holy angels.

We all recognise the wisdom of loyalty to the boss, and Jesus is the boss above all. He reminds us that he's coming back to resurrect us all to face his judgment. If we've been loyal to him and his gospel—faithfully believing, proclaiming and contending for the gospel of "Christ crucified"—he will be loyal to us. He will never forget us. He will come and take us home. But if we abandon him and his gospel, he will abandon us to hell, which he described as living in flames—not because God is a torturer, but because God in his holiness is a consuming fire.

We will sometimes fail, make selfish decisions or be too afraid to speak up. This is what Peter did in denying Jesus on the night when Jesus was arrested. But Peter was repentant. Jesus in grace and patience reassures Peter and all of us who fail and repent that we are still forgiven and useful to our Lord in his mission. Jesus' purpose for our lives is clear, whoever we are and however much we stumble: to follow him down the way of the cross in living for the salvation of others.

As we conclude, it's worth observing that living with this purpose, for all our talk of sacrifice, is surprisingly fulfilling. Living for the salvation of others is deeply satisfying, because it is the Christ-like lifestyle for which we were created.

Probably the most famous of all lifeboat sailors is the legendary Dick Evans, who operated from Moelfre in Anglesey, North Wales, for almost 50 years. He won the first of his gold medals for his bravery in the rescue of the *Hindlea* in October 1959. In mountainous seas and hurricane winds, Evans ten times steered his little lifeboat close to the stricken vessel so that the exhausted crew could jump onto the lifeboat. After the rescue Evans reported, "I sat on the slipway utterly exhausted. Suddenly I realised that tears were streaming down my face. They were tears of joy. My crew and I had saved eight men from a certain death and I felt very happy about it."

I'm not surprised! The joy of bringing people to Christ is just like that.

Even last week, one of my staff came into my study with those same tears of joy streaming down his face. He recounted how over recent days he'd had the privilege of reading the Scriptures to his dying father, before leading him in a prayer of commitment to Jesus in the last days of his life. There is surely no greater joy than bringing people to Jesus for salvation.

The legendary missionary Hudson Taylor, who suffered extreme privations in his mission to the unreached millions of China, is said to have declared boldly, "I never made a sacrifice for Jesus". He was testifying that denying ourselves and taking up our cross to follow Jesus, however costly, feels like a joyful privilege even when it's a painful sacrifice. Because following Jesus along the way of the cross means not only living a life full of rewarding purpose in leading people to salvation—but it also means living close to him.

Why not turn to Jesus now in prayer?

Thank him for dying for you on that cross.

Thank him for setting you free from slavery to sin.

Thank him for forgiving you.

Thank him for justly qualifying you for heaven with his righteous life.

Thank him for calling you to follow him.

Ask him for the courage and strength of his Holy Spirit to deny yourself, take up your cross and follow him on the way of the cross, ready to suffer cost for the salvation of others.

Or just thank him for the cross in four words: freedom, forgiveness, justice and purpose.

QUESTIONS FOR DISCUSSION

1. How does it change our experience of church to think of it as a cruise ship, a battleship, or a lifeboat?

2. What are the differences and similarities between Jesus' mission and our mission?

3. What experiences have you had of the cost of proclaiming the cross?

4. What is most challenging or exciting for you about Jesus' purpose for our lives?

5. Which of the four illustrations of the benefit of following Jesus—savings, investments, currency, and loyalty—do you find most compelling?

6. What could you do this week to deny yourself, take up your cross, and follow Jesus? What could you plan to do over the coming year?

7. Which non-Christian friends, family members or communities could you commit to praying for regularly?

CONTRIBUTORS

RICHARD COEKIN

Richard is CEO of the London-wide Co-Mission church-planting network and Senior Pastor of Dundonald Church in south-west London. The author of several books including *Our Father* and *Gospel DNA*, Richard is married to Sian and they have five children.

KEVIN DEYOUNG

Kevin is the Senior Pastor at Christ Covenant Church in Matthews, North Carolina, and Assistant Professor of Systematic Theology at Reformed Theological Seminary. Kevin is married to Trisha and they have eight children. He is the author of a number of books, including *Just Do Something* and *The Hole In Our Holiness*.

YANNICK CHRISTOS-WAHAB

Yannick was born and raised in London, where he still lives, and is Pastor of Stockwell Baptist Church. He is married to Kiitan and loves sports, theology and talking to people.

BIBLICAL | RELEVANT | ACCESSIBLE

At The Good Book Company, we are dedicated to helping Christians and local churches grow. We believe that God's growth process always starts with hearing clearly what he has said to us through his timeless word—the Bible.

Ever since we opened our doors in 1991, we have been striving to produce Bible-based resources that bring glory to God. We have grown to become an international provider of user-friendly resources to the Christian community, with believers of all backgrounds and denominations using our books, Bible studies, devotionals, evangelistic resources, and DVD-based courses.

We want to equip ordinary Christians to live for Christ day by day, and churches to grow in their knowledge of God, their love for one another, and the effectiveness of their outreach.

Call us for a discussion of your needs or visit one of our local websites for more information on the resources and services we provide.

Your friends at The Good Book Company

thegoodbook.com | thegoodbook.co.uk
thegoodbook.com.au | thegoodbook.co.nz
thegoodbook.co.in